At Gloaming

Poems by Larry Schug

Also by Larry Schug and published by North Star Press:

Scales Out of Balance: Poems by Lawrence Schug (1990)
Caution: Thin Ice: Poems by Lawrence Schug (1993)
The Turning of Wheels: Poems by Larry Schug (2001)
Arrogant Bones: Poems by Larry Schug (2008)
Nails: Poems by Larry Schug (2011)

AT GLOAMING

POEMS BY LARRY SCHUG

NORTH STAR PRESS OF ST. CLOUD, INC.
St. Cloud, Minnesota

Dedicated to Juli
There is no poetry without you.

Front cover photo: Larry Schug
Author photo: Juliann Rule

First Edition: March 2014

Printed in the United States of America

Published by
North Star Press of St. Cloud, Inc.
P.O. Box 451
St. Cloud, MN 56302
northstarpress.com

ACKNOWLEDGEMENTS

The following poems or versions thereof were originally published in the following print or electronic journals or anthologies. Thank you to all the editors, patrons and readers of these publications.

"Nude Modeling" and "The Implications of Washing Dishes" in *Studio 1*.

"Etched in Granite" and "Sharon Springs, Kansas" in *The Talking Stick*.

"Thanks, Dude," "The Lights Go off During the Super Bowl," "In Light Of," "A Place Called Ghost Ranch," "Green Heron in Rain," "You Wish," "A Speculation on Spiders," and "The Killdeer Response" in *Wild Goose Poetry Review*.

"Runaway Tractor" in *Bareback Magazine*.

"A Small Kindness, This" and "Apple Harvest" in *Chantarelle's Notebook*.

"The Burden of Souls" and "Wood Ticks, That's Different" in *Cynic Café*.

"An Accordion, I Think" and "At the Arboretum" in *River Poet's Journal*.

"Between the Lines" in *Matchbook*.

"Mending Mittens," and "Rhubarb" in *Your Daily Poem*.

"Everyone Forgot" in *Misfits' Miscellaneous*.

"Dull Knife's Blanket" and "Ghost Warriors" in *Trajectory*.

"Fish" in *Imitation Fruit*.

"Pretender," "The Perfect Time," "Apprentice Gods" and "Conjecture" in *Circle Show*.

"Homeless in Duluth," "Toads," and "Memorial" in *Nota Bene*.

"This Beautiful Air" in *New Plains Review*.

"Sailors Becalmed," "A Dream of Roger Young," "You Could Fool Yourself," and "One Way to Bridge a Cultural Divide" in *Main Channel Voices*.

"At Gloaming" in *Poetry Quarterly*.

"A Lesson in Mindfulness" in *A Year of Being Here*.

TABLE OF CONTENTS

I. An Invisible Thread

II. Just This Side of Invisible

III. When the TV's Turned Off

I
AN INVISIBLE THREAD

Light, as a Feather

Amenable to spells, omens,
talismans, totems,
to simple beauty,
I pick up a black feather,
a tatter of night
fallen from a raven's cape;
become mesmerized by the prism of colors
it casts, this ebony feather
of no more or less mystical property
than anything else fallen from the sky,
yet intensely significant as the feather it is,
twirling between my fingertips,
catching and releasing light born of darkness.

Watch Yourself around Crows

Everybody knows crows talk
Crawk Crawk
don't need no subpoena
to start a raucous squawkin'
Don't be fooled by a crow's
drunken sailor walk
watch yourself
crows ain't tattlers or tale tellers
witnesses what they be
sayin' it like they see it
keepin' an ebony eye on the world

The Killdeer Response

Feigning a broken wing,
a killdeer tries to lure me away
from her nest of stones,
spotted eggs hidden within.
She recognizes me for what I am—
a predator,
and though I have no intention of harm,
my presence alarms her,
ignites a primordial response,
the same response your mother would have
to a stranger lurking near your house
when you were a nestling.

Great Blue Heron

A great blue heron
hunting leopard frogs
stands stick-still in green muck,
one leg tucked into its breast,
crested head poised like an arrow
notched in a drawn bowstring.

I see that silence and intensity
do not guarantee the heron a meal;
patience is not always rewarded.
Sometimes it becomes necessary
to fly to another pond,
hungry.

A Lesson in Mindfulness

A Buddhist monk
is trying to teach me
mindfulness
from a book
but my stomach
is too full of ice cream
for me to breathe properly.

Outside my window,
a hungry green heron,
perched perfectly still,
fully in his moment,
surveys the pond
for frogs and fish.
The teacher
has grown green wings,
the book having folded up
its feathers for the night.

Green Heron in Rain

The light's not right, too much glare
for a photo through the rain-streaked window,
and not being a painter or sketcher
I turn to words to capture and convey
the image of a solitary green heron,
its rusty breast, pointed crest, stiletto beak,
preening gray-green feathers worn like a cape;
gripping a branch of a fallen aspen
with long feet, orange as a prairie sunset.
The steel-gray pond bubbles and ripples in the rain,
backdrop of shimmering quicksilver,
a scene that could move an agnostic soul
to believe in the hand of some god
with no religion to muddy the image,
within or without.

Ripples

Each ripple created as geese take flight
reflects its own sunset,
ripple follows ripple, sunset follows sunset
like days follow days, adding up to a life,
your life.
You may see your life in this bruised sky
of royal purple and tangerine, citrean yellow.
When the water calms, slips into sleep,
that's your life, too,
reflected in dreams of starshine.

Sandhill Cranes

From the periphery of vision
on a moving bicycle,
the three sandhill cranes look like deer,
feathers, the same cinnamon color
deer don in early summer, catching sun;
their postures, long necks bent
to the ground like grazing deer,
before I notice the rose-colored berets
they wear, as they lift their heads
from a low spot in an alfalfa field,
looking down long beaks, warily watching me.
I slow, pedal past them quietly as I can,
out of respect, perhaps reverence
for their magnificence of essence,
fear for how perilous is their existence,
thankful for proof of being, cranes and mine,
as we each acknowledge the other, eyes meeting.

Clouds

A bushy-browed old man
chases a white poodle
across a blue meadow
though he knows
white clouds won't return
any more than his youth
or bad dogs will,
no matter how loud he rumbles.

Fluffy!
Damn you, Fluffy;
you get your ass back here.
Come on, Fluffy, dang you.
Fluffy! Fluffy!

Rain Delay

         rain
         rain
         rain
         rain

         rain
              delay
rain   delay
       rain delay
         rain delay
           rain delay
rain delay rain delay rain delay
  raindelay raindelay raindelay
raindelayraindelayraindelayraindelay
     delay delay delay
       rain rain rain
    delay rain delay rain
       delay
               rain
        rain
       rain
     de   lay
       rain
  de   lay

     Play Ball!

February Blue

It's February 23rd, a Saturday,
in Avon, Minnesota;
the snow is "up to my ass" deep,
but the sky is blue, February blue,
a shade paler than June blue,
but full with promise of Spring.
If I position myself just so
at my writing table, all I see is sky.
With the first spring training game
playing on the radio,
I imagine a towering fly ball
climbing into my field of blue vision,
I imagine a centerfielder in Florida,
palm trees waving in a warm wind
beyond the outfield fence,
pulling his sunglasses over his eyes,
pounding his glove three times
before gathering in that fly ball
like people believe god gathers in souls,
never making an error.

Sharon Springs, Kansas

The sky blows like a blue blanket
hanging on a clothesline
on the outskirts of Sharon Springs,
a horizon you'll never reach
even at eighty miles an hour;
and you don't care
because you're from Minnesota,
where you're always looking inward,
the tall trees holding up their arms,
blocking every horizon,
preventing you from seeing
too far ahead or behind.
You think if you awoke
under a sky this wide
every morning of your life,
things would be different with you.

Moon Haiku

a crescent moon hangs
in ethereal blue sky
miracle of light

This Pale Moon Floating

It's just the view
from my point of view,
just geometry, really,
the work of gravity,
this pale moon,
barely visible,
floating in blue sky.
Mathematics could explain the moon
moving in its orbit of the planet,
but math can't explain beauty,
the stirring of tides in the soul,
why I call a crescent moon ethereal,
light, a miracle.
Poetry doesn't explain it either,
though poetry reveals
what knowledge conceals.

Tango Luna

What if
instead of playing golf,
the astronauts would have danced
on the moon;
done clumsy pirouettes in bulky spacesuits,
simple box steps
kicking up moon dust in starlight
instead of just that one giant step?

A slicing golf ball, even hit on the moon
inspires no one.
They could've danced a lunar tango
in blue-green earthlight,
leaving a pattern of intricate footprints
that would've set everyone on our little planet
dancing the same dance,
the way we used to when the moon was full.

While Watching the Leonid Meteor Shower

I'm lying on the lawn,
head propped on a stone,
while Orion stalks the Great Bear,
Sirius, the star dog, at his side.
They pay no heed to burning meteors,
shaken like rain from the lion's mane.
I envy the Sky Hunter his long life,
while in the brief flashes of fiery dust,
I see how quickly my small life passes.
My old dog wonders what the hell
he's doing out here at 3:00 a.m.,
yet he lies down in the grass,
curls up beside me, unquestioning,
loyal as any star dog.
After watching this cosmic light show,
I come to the thought
that it's not important how long a light shines;
the wonder is that there is light at all.

Working Women

It's only been recently
that 7-11s
have occupied the same universe
as the Pleiades sisters and Cassiopeia.
I'd like to think these women,
luminous and heavenly beauties,
cook thoughtfully and organically,
wouldn't just stop and pick up
some microwave enchiladas for dinner
while gassing up their cars
after the commute home from work,
but as the old bard once said,
in paraphrase, that is,
there's a lot more goin' down
than we'll ever know, eh?

Cat as Zen Master

The weather report on the radio,
the radar display on the computer screen,
the roiling clouds beyond the tamaracks
signal heavy rain, lightning, thunder and wind.
The cat knows this as well as I do,
though his information comes from sources
to which I have no access.
He sleeps with his head on the window sill,
unconcerned, practicing Zen Master that he is,
living in the present, as always,
while I fret about working in the rain tomorrow,
trees falling on the roof tonight,
hail stones shredding the garden my wife loves so much.

Hail Storm

A hail storm flattened your garden,
shredded rhubarb leaves and lilies,
icy shrapnel exploded tomatoes,
snapped pea vines, pelted pumpkins,
shriveled the bounteous harvest
you'd been visualizing
since sowing seeds in spring's cool loam.
And though you mourn,
you bend back to work,
nursing and nurturing what remains,
with tender hands and tears in your eyes,
the way I know you'll take care of me
no matter the storms ahead.

Evanescence

The sky is gray and white
as a nuthatch;
evanescent pink blossoms
blow off crabapple trees
like all the innocent
iridescent lives
that will fall today
all over the world,
absorbed like snowflakes
by the warm earth,
leaving a lingering sweetness,
a hope for apples.

The Same Beautiful Air

My wife asleep beside me,
two cats sharing the bed with us,
the dog lying on the floor,
a Christmas cactus near the window
and we're all breathing
each others' breaths,
sharing the same beautiful air
breathed by every other being
on this atmospheric planet.
And you know what that means.

A Speculation on Spiders

A great spider spins an invisible thread,
weaves an invisible web,
ties together every thing, every where, every when.
No one knows the entirety of this web,
where it hangs, what lies between its threads.
We perceive ourselves existing
in one time, in one place, on one strand,
but if we pay attention we feel a vibration,
music in the humming string to which we cling.
Some seek the spider,
some hide from her,
but no one can escape this web,
these shining, singing, silver strands.

Spider

takes no notice of me
bending over her weaving.
She weaves her way inward,
attaches silken cables to silken spokes,
spins a seat at wheel's hub,
waits for silver strings to sing.

Toads

In May
when it's finally warm enough
to open bedroom windows,
toads sing all night,
voices hypnotic as choral bells.
I wish I didn't need to sleep,
but the amphibians' songs
become a lullaby,
then a soundtrack for dreams.
I open my eyes at first light,
the chorus of toads still singing,
and I'm not really sure
if I'm awake or still asleep,
alive or dead.
Perhaps we exist in all these states at once.
Perhaps being is a song we sing to ourselves.
Perhaps we are the song itself.

A Serpent's Lament

Give me a break!
I'm not a metaphor
I'm just a snake,
a serpent,
a creature of god, same as you;
friendly, all in all,
though I keep to myself.
To prove my good intentions,
I gave your wife an apple,
a beautiful, shiny fruit, finest on the tree,
that contains all you need to know to get by.
And what do I get in return?
Bad press—
the image of a slimy, slithering, hissy monster,
vipery, venomous, virulent,
something to be feared, killed if caught,
driven into the Irish Sea, for god's sake.
How can you blame me
if I lose it now and again, bite somebody.
Give me a break.
I'm just a snake.

Wood Ticks

I know a woman who captures spiders
inside her house, then releases them
outside, unharmed;
she allows ladybugs
to huddle in a little orange ball
in a tall corner of the ceiling all winter.
She wouldn't squish a spider,
but she picks ticks off her dog
or her own body
or mine
and flushes them down the toilet,
though she thinks they survive the ride,
like little body surfers, through the pipes
leading to the septic tank,
and she thinks the ticks
crawl out the tank's vent pipe,
creep through the grass, looking for blood.

The Isle Royale Wolf Pack

A scenario no one imagined,
that the end could begin this way;
the alpha male, another male,
and one the island's two females
taking an entire ecosystem with them
as they fell through a fragile crust of ice,
mystery and mystique disappearing with them,
into an old mine shaft, abandoned in 1853,
leaving a single she-wolf in a hopeless pack.
Stars shine on trackless snow;
a song without a chorus sung
on the longest winter nights.
Even the island's moose,
pawing for grass beneath crusted snow,
may feel a nameless emptiness
at the absence of a song
that fills them with fear.

Cascade Falls

The waterfall seems to say
I wish   I wish   I wish
but I wonder if it's the water speaking
or that voice in my head,
always wishing for something,
trying to cast a spell or blessing
on the two of us
because we have the audacity
to walk in this slippery stream
on feet made of clay.

Cascade River

Below the falls
the river riffles and warbles,
goes on and on
about how it has to run off,
though it dearly loves
the smooth skins
of these boulders and stones
it's been polishing
since the glacier's retreat.

Bottled Water

A hot wind wicks away the water
from a person's skin,
empties the aquifer of internal water, too,
after it takes the surface lake of sweat.
Replenish, replenish,
the experts say,
eight glasses a day—
advice only for the fortunate
who have no need to carry water
from a sporadic seep
or a polluted well ten miles away;
wait in line at a tanker truck
in a refugee camp
with a chance the truck may run dry
while waiting with a jug full of dust
and nothing they can say to their children
while the person in front of them
is happy to be getting the tank's dregs
for her babies to drink.
Ever think of that when you turn on the tap
or twist off the cap of the bottled water
you bought to quench a thirst
that is the mere drying of morning dew
on the shore of a vast lake?

At Gloaming

Watching four deer
come out of the woods at gloaming,
graze in a pasture, purple
with alfalfa flowers and twilight,
a woman, finally able to sit a minute,
breathes the sweet evening;
her sleeping children, awake in her thoughts,
bringing their own kind of peace.
Words are not needed,
though some might call this moment tranquil,
poetry.

Conjecture

The doe's back was raked raw,
claw marks, it seems,
but what would do such a thing, and how?
A cougar, I conjecture,
leaping from a limb onto her back,
but how did she shake it off
and why no bite marks on her neck?

I wonder, was that same doe
the matted pile of hide
and scattered bones I found
when the snow melted?
And why did she return to memory
six years later—
a kind of re-birth for the sake of a poem,
a lesson in mortality sent by some local god?

A Small Kindness, This

An anonymous passerby,
someone on their way to work,
perhaps some bicyclist,
took the time to remove the cat,
hit by a car in the night, from the roadway,
place it in the ditch among wild violets
before more tires, feasting crows,
and other agents of decay
could begin their work on the carcass;
a small kindness, this,
to foster a measure of dignity
during these times of anonymous death,
unmarked graves.

Maple Syrup Time

With a blessing we enter the woods,
trudging through fresh-fallen snow,
knee-deep and sparkling, rejoicing
under sky the color of a bluejay's wing;
tree markers, drillers, tappers,
bucket hangers and harvesters,
humbly and gratefully reaping the gift
of soil and water and sun
given us by acer saccharum,
the generous sugar maples,
casting their shadows,
like a forest of sundials on settled snow,
telling us it's time for making maple syrup!

No Help

October's golden tamaracks
return yellow light to the sun,
clear water gives back blue
borrowed from the sky.
A luxurious mink,
fur, wet and glistening,
bursts onto the scene,
a cameo appearance,
a teaser, suggesting purpose of being
as it rustles through dry cattails,
a destination seemingly in mind,
so unlike browsing deer
moving from one green leaf to the next,
the way so many people
seem to move about their lives.
Though there are many theories
as to its pertinence,
there seems to be no help
from the producer or director of this scene,
left to the viewer to find whatever meaning,
if any, there is to be found in blatant mystery.

Apprentice Gods

We spend the afternoon
rolling rocks down a sandy scree slope
at the base of Orphan Mesa,
laughing like little children
as the stones tumble and jump
until lying still as gravestones
when gravity exhausts itself on level ground.
We play at rearranging the landscape
as if we are apprentice gods, practicing on stones
before learning to stir water and wind
into floods and hurricanes,
shake the earth into quaking, just for a laugh.
Tomorrow, we decide,
we'll plant trees and heal the scars of erosion,
maybe pick up trash along the highway
on our continuing quest for divinity.

Mending Mittens

Mending my leather mittens
for the third time this winter,
I sew them with waxed string
made to repair fishing nets,
hoping they'll last
until the splitting maul rests
against the shrunken woodpile
and the hoe and spade come out of the shed.
I find myself praying.
Blessed be those who have laced together
the splits at the seams of this world,
repair its threads of twisted waters.
Blessed be those who stitch together
the animals and the land,
repair the rends in the fabric
of wolf and forest,
of whale and ocean,
of condor and sky.
Blessed be those who are forever fixing
the tear between people and the rest of life.
May we all have enough thread,
may our needles be sharp,
may our fingers not throb or go numb.
May each of us find an apprentice,
someone who will take the needle from our hands,
continue all the mending that needs to be done.

At the Arboretum

This summer day is a woman
wearing a blue bonnet, green slippers
and a floral print dress;
she tends to beds of black-eyed susans, blue-eyed grass,
purple coneflowers and climbing clematis,
a garden of phlox, ox-eye daisies;
a bower of blue spruce, Japanese yews,
chestnuts, walnuts, butternuts and hickories,
a lawn of pampas grass and sarsaparilla.
This day, I spend with two women who love me,
each in their own way;
two women I love,
each in their own way.
One brings me wild rice,
one pays for my lunch.
I can't comprehend any of it—
the way earth and flower
eat each other, but neither dies.
I don't understand love, either;
that comes in as many colors and shapes and aromas
as flowers in a garden, trees in a woods, grasses on the prairie.

Grasses Rustling

Beauty has become an app
in an oxymoronic place
called virtual reality.
Thoughtful thought is passé,
lost among bits and bytes;
truth is subjective, irrelevant.
And poetry,
oh god, dear, dear poetry
doesn't know it's dead
among the corpses of words unsaid,
goes on being written in grasses rustling,
spoken by the wind.

Coneflowers

Prairie coneflowers
purple and yellow
petals hanging
like the folded umbrellas
on a closed bistro patio
attract honey bees
and monarch butterflies
cruising the cafés
beneath turquoise sky
sampling nectars
like lonely lovers looking
for amor

An Accordion, I Think
(A poem of privilege on a good day)

I've got all the sunrise my eyes can gather.
Every time I need a breath of air,
it's there;
and every time I need to exhale a stale breath
I just do it
and there's a place for it to go.
When I am thirsty, there is water,
all manner and mixture of foods for when I hunger;
black-eyed susans, blue-eyed grass
swaying in a puff of wind
when nothing else will soothe me.
I hear you downstairs;
you don't sing or shuffle your feet,
but I hear music,
an accordion, I think.

Juli and Blue Violets

My task is to paint you
and blue violets,
all abloom on the wood's edge,
the splash of sunlight on your face,
your hair, a tangled weave
of fallen maple leaves.

I will paint you on a poet's page,
with subtle shades,
and I will paint shadows
and tall grasses
where I can hide,
a spy who would reveal
the secrets you conceal.

Rhubarb

By April, sour red stalks
push elephant-ear leaves
into near-earth atmosphere.
Rhubarb plans ahead,
years, decades even,
lives sustainably on the interest
of sunlight stored underground,
having folded up its solar collectors
in September,
when the days grow too short
to make sugar.
See how simple is a miracle.

Thoughts in the Rhubarb Patch

The president interrupted programming
to announce that we killed the terrorist.
Ding dong, the witch is dead—
the people are rejoicing,
waving flags with a vengeance,
but it doesn't mean much in the rhubarb patch.
Violence begets violence,
death begets death;
it seems no excuse for a dance.
Sunlight begets rhubarb,
rhubarb begets pie,
which seems more reason for celebration
than perpetual retaliation,
an eye for an eye for an eye,
ad infinitum.

You Could Fool Yourself

If you fold up your paper,
turn off your radio and TV,
sit on the steps and sip your tea,
watch the birds and speak no words
as the sun rises yellow and round,
making rainbows on the dewy lawn,
you could fool yourself into thinking
there's no bloody war going on.

II
Just This Side of Invisible

Caucasian

I'm classified as Caucasian
by government agencies
though I have never been
to the Caucasus Mountains
or Asia, for that matter,
but judging by the tint of my skin,
the shape of my face, I can guess
that somewhere in pre-European mist,
a peasant woman was raped by a soldier
in the army of one of the great Khans,
swooping into her village on horseback,
burning it to the ground,
killing her husband, father and brothers.
Perhaps that's why I dream of horses,
know that nothing I have,
not even the blood in my veins,
has not been stolen from someone.

Vinegar

There was nothing either of them said or could say
that night they saw so much of themselves in each other.
He saw himself in the boy behind bars
and from the son's point of view,
his old man was locked up too.
At times like this we tend to think in clichés—
what goes around comes around.
The pain they gave, maybe each figured they deserved
when it was given back to them,
though neither of them meant it to be like this.

But her? She didn't deserve what she got
from the two people she loved the most.
She stuck with them, her love cured them,
but she didn't live long enough
to see their best years together.
It's always too late for sorry,
but sorry doesn't go away.
The old man took his sorry to the grave
while his son lives with a heart full of sorry
and only ghosts to tell it to,
having learned how time vinegars sorry into sorrow.

Like Father, Like Son

The odor of stale smoke and alcohol
enters my bedroom before daylight.
My father wakes me with a whisper,
softly squeezes my shoulder,
gently brushes my cheek,
the way you might expect
a barber's hand would touch you.

I pretend I'm asleep;
my father pretends with me,
each of us trying to reconcile
the night before.
He knows he kept me from sleeping
him and that whiskey;
the fighting with my mother.
I can feel his guilt and shame
and I know he knows I've been crying,
but we don't say a word about it,
so like each other that way.

Me and Jimmy

We got no driving lessons from our fathers,
no advice on how to negotiate the pot-holed streets;
they just put us behind the wheel, told us to go,
and so we drove, pretending the road was smooth,
like it seemed to be for everyone else.
We ignored the ruts of hurt and bitterness,
the bumps of isolation we felt,
paved them over with self-delusion, false bravery,
thinking that if we turned the radio up loud enough
we could cruise down the road that shook us,
barely hanging on to the wheel,
each so ashamed of our own white knuckles, wide eyes,
we couldn't admit them even to each other
because we were brought up by fathers
who didn't talk about what they felt in their hearts,
both of us afraid of running head on into our drunken old man,
out of control again, swerving into our lane.

The Allman Brothers Singing
(For B.)

We hear the song from an empty street,
The Allman Brothers singing
"You're my blue sky,
You're my sunny day."
The song draws us to a joint so dark
we can't see each others' faces.
We order beers,
though beer would kill us in waking life,
your soul, my body.
I wake before the bartender
can pull back the handle on the tap,
saving both of us,
not the way the blues usually ends.

My Mother Crying

I remember that it was snowing,
cold enough in the house
we melted the frost on the window
with our hand prints
to see the car that stopped in the street,
the man from the church coming to the door
carrying a frozen turkey.
I don't remember
if my father was in the hospital, sick,
or in the other hospital, drying out.
I remember my mother crying,
then calling her sisters,
and that the next day, Thanksgiving,
the house was crowded with cousins,
aunts and uncles, but absent my father.
I remember how quiet was the house
that evening after everyone had left
and I lay in bed with my brother,
unable to sleep, my mother crying,
alone in her bed.

Angels

Teary-eyed, Mom said
God needed another angel;
that's why he took my baby sister,
all of ten days old.
Another angel; it made sense to me,
just a child, myself.

She stayed in her room days on end;
we heard her crying and did our best
to be good boys.
We played outside all day,
made snow angels all over the yard,
some outside mother's window,
our way of showing love and sadness
and trying to offer comfort, I suppose.

Wet and cold, when we came inside,
we ate the soup Mom had heated up for us;
She brushed the snow from wings
only she could see,
a different kind of tear
rolling down her cheek, just then.

Kisses

I

I was there, hovering somewhere
over the horizon of their first kiss,
that first real kiss,
the kiss where my father got lost,
forgot every lonely moment of his orphaned past;
realized this touch of lip to lip, tongue to tongue,
was the beginning of a new life
where he could finally settle.

II

I sat in the back seat with my little brother
that Saturday Mom drove us down to Willmar
to pick up Dad from the "hospital"
where he went to dry out.
She told him she loved him,
was so proud of him;
how life would be better now.
She was all over him, kissing him in the car
like we'd never seen them kiss.
Young boys, we were embarrassed, I guess,
by this show of overt affection.
Mom just laughed, kissed him some more,
then turned around and kissed us, too,
while Dad drove us all home,
somehow keeping his hands on the wheel
and the back seat suddenly became crowded
with five more yet-to-be born babies.

III

It was a lingering peck on the cheek,
a goodnight kiss,
though it's hard to really kiss someone,
with all those tubes in the way,
those monitors blinking,
your wife barely breathing.
When the phone rang late at night,
he answered with a trembling voice,
afraid of what he knew he would hear.
He kissed her one more time,
her skin cold against his lips.
Every night during his last years,
after his tears had dried,
he kissed her in his dreams
and, sometimes, he swore,
she kissed him in return.

Andy Williams Died Today

After a day of waitressing,
my mother came home and waited on her family;
then late at night, finally off her tired feet,
she'd wind down by reading romance novels,
smoking cigarettes, drinking coffee
while listening to those clean-cut crooners hippies hated,
Dean Martin, Perry Como, Vic Damone,
Andy Williams, her favorite,
on the old cabinet stereo, turned down low.
If there is a heaven, I'm pretty sure my mom's there,
and I hope Andy Williams is there now, too.
And I hope some angel perched on Andy's shoulder,
will whisper in Andy's ear, ask him to croon
"Moon River" for my mother.

The Old Guys at Kay's Kitchen

The old guys, the "regulars,"
sit in the same corner booth every morning,
comfortable as brothers with each other,
coffee cups in hand,
laughing like children one minute,
becoming loud when old arguments surface,
then going silent as stones when talk turns
to their war or old friends passing.

Four old friends and I, newly retired,
gather at Kay's for lunch today.
I see us as if from outside, how we must appear
to the young working guys eating their lunch,
and I realize that to them
we're the old guys in the corner booth
as we reminisce about old ballplayers,
our war, friends gone too soon.

We're the old guys.
I say it to myself, we're the old guys,
though we've not admitted this to ourselves.
I wonder how this could be possible,
that the years have left so many footprints
on the fading trail behind us.
We bask in the warmth of each others' presence,
knowing something we could not know yesterday.

this young guy,
workin' dude, I'd guess,
cap on backward,
sleeves ripped off his t-shirt at the shoulders,
just being respectful,
true to good upbringing,
holds open the door of the Holiday store
for an old guy I see reflected in the glass.
It's me. Holy crap, it's me.
I'm an old guy.
When did it happen that people open doors
for me?
I can open my own god damn door.
I'm the one who holds doors open for old folks.
I think, I'm gonna tell that young pup
what's up and I do;
I walk past him;
right next to the Nut Goodies
I nod once,
whisper like a truck on gravel.

Thanks, Dude

Diagnosis

On the same day
the doctor called with my lab results,
one of the old sisters at the convent
told me about the fate of an eighty-year-old maple,
just a sapling when she entered the sisterhood,
standing beside a building just as old,
scheduled for demolition, unsavable
with faulty wiring, leaky plumbing, crumbling brick.
That maple tree's got to go, she said,
its insides are as rotten as that building's
and it's in the way of new construction.

I didn't tell her about my failing infrastructure,
my withering leaves, disintegrating heartwood.
I haven't come to terms with it, myself;
and though my demise is not as imminent
as that of the old building or maple tree,
and it won't be a wrecking ball
or screaming chainsaw that takes me down,
the earth's pull on my transient and evanescent bones
feels suddenly stronger today, more insistent.

Sailors Becalmed

I try to summon enough wind
to fill both our sails,
but have barely enough breath
to keep my own sail full.
I fear losing sight of you,
becalmed in my wake
as I ride a fickle wind
over the horizon, knowing
that even if I drop my sails,
I can't give you the breath
that propels me on my journey,
it blows for my sail alone.
The best I can do is drop anchor,
wait with you as your ship sinks,
keep you afloat in my memory.

Memorial

Spirits are conjured in these songs you loved,
sung by your friends—
a Tennessee stud horse,
a Mexican cook named Ben;
even Frodo, the three-legged dog,
comes limping out of the past
when called by a poem.
But this night belongs to you, old friend,
remembered as you'd have liked—
a barn dance, not a wake,
your ashes blasted starward by a fireworks rocket,
exploding as a fountain of light eclipsing the moon.
Many people report seeing you tonight,
returning when the poet speaks your name,
when the singers sing their songs for you.
I see you at the periphery of the gathering,
at the edge of the bonfire, seated on a hay bale,
just this side of invisible,
not quite here, not quite not here.
Your presence is pervasive,
though the fiddler's dog sleeps peacefully
beside the fiddler's tapping toe,
paying no attention to you at all.

From All Appearances

Roger's family and friends
gather together on the bank
of La Prairie River,
remember him
with stories and songs,
poems and prayers.
Roger is the only one here
who, from all appearances,
is not here,
though his presence is pervasive.
It makes me wonder
who else that isn't here,
is here.

A Dream of Roger Young

Old friend,
thank you for visiting last night,
and for bringing our long-gone dogs,
Pluto and Frodo, with you
for a romp in a sun-dappled wood,
a splash in a singing creek,
as we relived old times.
I know how busy you must be
with so many dreams to enter,
so many people missing you.
And I know it won't be long
before I join you,
seeking sleeping lovers and friends,
just to remind them to remember us
as they wake with bemused smiles,
bittersweet light in their hearts.

A Poem at Ann's Passing

On the day of Ann's passing
crabapple trees dress in pink blossoms,
each petal seemingly illuminated from within.
Cat birds and cardinals sing their mating songs—
glorious warbles sung with urgency and soul.

On the night of Ann's passing
moonlight is eclipsed by shadow,
the way the light dimmed in her eyes;
but then, moonlight is re-kindled,
the moon continues its journey
like a shining spirit set free.

Apple blossoms, song birds, return when they should,
moonlight always triumphs over darkness.
We are bequeathed beauty, song and light,
to furnish the house where memory dwells.
Let us share this softening of our hearts.

Blueberry Muffins

She left a bowl of blueberries
on the kitchen counter,
went to the post office with her husband,
just to ride along.
How was she to know
he wouldn't see the flashing light,
that she'd never get back
to add flour, sugar, milk and eggs,
baking powder, salt and soda?
She'd never have left the kitchen
in such a mess if she had known.

The day of her funeral
her children are milling around in the kitchen;
the counter and kitchen table covered
with cakes and pies and six kinds of cookies
brought over by the neighbors,
but everyone here hungers
for one of her blueberry muffins.

Pretender

The widow turns on the kitchen radio,
tunes it to a ballgame while she watches TV.
The radio bothers the hell out of her,
just like it did when her husband was alive.
But after the ballgame and her shows are over,
when she turns the distractions off at bedtime,
the house is so quiet;
she's the only one in their double bed
and there's just no way
to pretend her way out of that.

Veteran

He returned from 'Nam,
discharged honorably, he was told,
though he didn't feel that way.
The first thing he did after disembarking in Minneapolis
was tear the name tag and medals from his uniform,
flush them down the toilet in the airport,
stuff his dress greens in a wastebasket,
change into his civvies
and smoke some of the grass he'd smuggled back
as he sat in a locked toilet stall.
His parents waited outside
and as he rode home in the back seat of the yellow Dodge
his mother talked about him going back to school,
his father, about where he might get a job.
He sat back, dazzled by the lights of "The World"
and wondered how he'd ever get all this blood off his hands
and why his parents couldn't see it, couldn't smell it.
Thirty years later, his parents have died;
he's been married three times,
has two daughters and a son who don't acknowledge him.
His legs hurt, his veins are shot, his words slurred from whiskey.
His hands shake, he can't walk a straight line
and yet he drives a beat-up car from one bar to the next,
caring only about the next drink,
hoping his disability check will last the month.
He keeps his bloody hands in his pockets.

Etched in Granite

Name after name of those who died
in a far-off jungle war are etched in granite,
a wall to justify death; the names,
those that politicians call fallen heroes.
But there is no wall, no memorial
for those who came home, eyes open,
bodies alive, souls dead,
got drunk and stayed that way thirty years,
strewing the wreckage of failed marriages
and neglected children in their wakes,
dead souls taking decades
to leave bodies ravaged by misery
married to guilt and shame.
On the wall I've built in my heart
I trace your name with my finger.

Lunch at Kay's Kitchen
(For Dan V. and Dan L.)

We were all so glad
you guys could join us for lunch,
though in spirit only, thanks to
Misters Kennedy, Johnson and Nixon.
You didn't need a menu,
didn't order a Rueben
or a plate of ribs,
didn't finish a meal with a slice
of Kay's famous rhubarb pie,
but you sat in the corner booth
with us in the same way
you live in the corners of our hearts.

The Mourners at "Shiner's" Funeral

are old, themselves;
many walk with canes,
some use walkers, some wheelchairs.
Some are aided by daughters
in their fifties or sixties,
who guide them through the ritual.
These old men and women
have lived in this town,
gone to this church all their lives;
they know exactly how it will be
four days after they die.

Fixing

Each nail and screw,
every nut and bolt and washer
is sorted by size,
stored in bins with its own kind.
All the hand tools
are hung on brackets in pegboard,
their outlines painted in white.
The tablesaw and sander
are pushed against the garage wall
and the workbench is clean
but for a single short one-by-two,
cut at a forty-five-degree angle,
a small pile of sawdust.
I wonder what he was making, repairing.
Did he die with a blueprint in his head,
buzzing around like snatches of poems inside mine?
Will someone find my notebook one day,
this jumble of symbols
that could be put together any which way,
try to make sense of it,
try to figure out what I was fixing?

Don't Forget

In a dream
my father knocked on my door.
He looked so good,
so real,
so alive.
Shocked, I stammered,
Dad, I thought you were . . .
Dead? I am, he said,
but I was feeling a little faded.
You've not been thinking of me.
I thought I'd pay you a visit.
It's true, you know;
the dead do live on
in the memories of the living.
Don't forget us.

III
WHEN THE TV'S TURNED OFF

Between Melancholy and Nostalgia

I want you to hear this poem
like you might hear a train in the night
an hour before you see the light
of its great diesel engine
rockin' through a vast grassland
where the dreams of coyotes
outnumber the dreams of people.
I want you to hear this poem
in your sleep.
I want this poem to wake you
so that you curse it,
so it puts a feeling in your stomach
somewhere between melancholy
and sweet nostalgia.
I want you to think of faces and places
that have come and gone
like a hundred-fifty boxcars
loaded with grain from a plowed-up prairie,
saw logs ripped from a mountain.
I want you to wake from a dream
you can't quite remember,
a dream that lingers
like a humming in steel tracks,
leaves you a little wobbly
when your feet first touch the floor.
That's how I want you to hear this poem.

Blame the Poem

Dead-ass tired by noon,
though not from shoveling snow,
digging out the car,
carrying in firewood,
all before breakfast.
I blame the poem
that woke me at 3:00 a.m.
like a dog whining
to be let out to piss.
It wouldn't let me be
until I got up and scribbled the words,
then kept whining and scratching
until I got it right.

Nude Modeling

I sit perfectly still,
bare naked, atop a stepladder,
my robe draped over a rung.
My ass is numb,
I stare dumbly at a crawling clock.
One pretty art student,
swishes charcoal in her sketchbook,
winks at me and laughs.
I feel movement
where anything but perfect stillness
would bring growing embarrassment.
But, I think, it could be worse.
If this was a poetry reading
I'd be baring my soul.

Dental Insurance

You just go to a dentist's office,
lie back in a reclining chair
and two beautiful women,
one black-haired, one blond,
give you laughing gas
and say Good night.
When you wake up
the pain of that ol' wisdom tooth
will be gone.
We'll give you some drugs
for the soreness.
Don't go to work tomorrow.

Apple Harvest

The apple tree in the backyard,
so heavy with Harelreds,
we need to prop up its limbs
with two-by-fours, one-by-sixes,
a length of old rain gutter,
a broken stepladder, shepherd's hooks,
whatever we can find
to keep the apples' weight from breaking branches.
Yet the branches droop lower every day.
To lighten their load, we pick some apples before they're ripe,
leave them in a pile on the ground,
a sacrificial offering to rabbits and raccoons,
to deer, in the hope they will leave some fruit to mature.

All this, and still the serpent is not appeased;
it picks the finest apple from the tree,
offers it to my wife,
who, in turn, offers it to me.
She has a look in her eyes I can't resist,
Eden be damned. I want what she proffers
though there is no end to the grief it will cause me
and now, I've been told,
any future apples must be earned by the sweat of my brow.

Everyone Forgot

A serpent, disguised as a girl,
went to school
with the fruit of the knowledge of good and evil
in her backpack.
She was gonna share it with her boyfriend,
but the teachers found it, ate the fruit first
and taught this knowledge to all their students
year after year after year.
Everyone believed in these teachings
but everyone forgot this knowledge
came from a serpent,
metaphorical though it was.
It wasn't long before
the teachers had killed all the snakes;
they had no choice, they said.

The Implications of Washing Dishes

You're washing dishes in water so hot
it turns your hands red, wrinkles your skin.
This implies you have
food
water
pots
pans
dishes
silverware
a sink
a residence.
This implies you ate today.
You're washing dishes—
two plates
two glasses
two knives
two forks
two spoons.
This implies
you're a lucky fucker, buckaroo.
You've got someone to eat with you.

When I Met You

My first job out of the army
was a paper route
delivering papers to paperboys.
I had this beater '61 Chevy pickup;
I put my dogs in back,
but they'd jump out at every stop,
following their noses into the neighborhoods.
I'd holler
"Barney! Frodo! God damn it, get back here!"
It was 2:00 or 3:00 a.m.,
they'd eventually come back to the truck
and luckily, nobody called the cops on us
for disturbing the peace of suburbia
or leaving dog shit on manicured lawns.
I usually rolled a couple joints
and had to add a quart of oil to the truck
to get through the route,
get back to the farm, go to sleep
with both dogs on the bed.
This all ended when I met you.

Sister Bay, Wisconsin

While we watch from the Irish café;
an old man in gray walks past the blue harbor,
sailboats rock at anchor, gentle as cradles,
gulls fly above, underbellies sunlit pink.
A green truck drives through this painting,
three black-and-white goats
perfectly balanced in its bed.
Our eyes turn from the window, meet
above the red-and-white-checkered tablecloth.
The morning holds all the promise of a kiss.

Winter

We leave our footprints in the snow,
our boots, just inside the door.
Caps, coats, mittens,
we hang beside the wood stove,
fling the rest
on the floor beside the bed
as we disrobe each other.
Your wooly sweater, your bra,
my red long johns, flannel shirt,
our socks, our jeans,
all touch, entwined,
but not dancing, possessing
none of the rhythm of our skins.

Lost Key

Panic stops my heart, I choke on my own breath
as I reach into an empty pocket.
I try another, another, every pocket,
then search them all again—no key.
I've lost the way to enter the house of your heart
after living there all these years;
I'd just assumed the door would always be unlocked,
that I could walk in anytime because I once gave you a rose.
But today the door would not yield,
you did not answer my knocking grown into pounding
and I don't blame you;
today I don't recognize myself, either.
I rifle through my pockets again,
in my mind, retrace my steps to doors I have opened
before today, thinking the key would be hanging
in one of the locks of yesterday's doors.
When I remember where the key has been left,
a sense of relief deflates me, leaves me shaking,
as I fear that you've changed the lock by now
because of the stranger who came to your door today,
the one who hopes to gain admittance with one yellow rose.

Fishing

Like fishermen,
we cast our prayers
into the sky, baited
with promises, praise and tears
to catch some god's attention,
and, then, with laughable arrogance
only humans possess,
we throw answered prayers
back into the sky
in hope of hooking a bigger fish
with our next cast.

Fish

He feels her eyes baiting him
as he leans against the car door,
thinking of fishing
as the scenery swims by.
Nothing she dangles
lures him out of deep water;
swimming around the minnow,
he refuses to bite,
afraid of being hooked, netted,
pulled into the suffocating atmosphere
inside the closed car,
though inside his silence
he is more afraid of the day
she puts away her lures.

Farm Girl

I dreamed I'd marry a farm boy
with a hay baler's shoulders
and a milker's soft hands.
But my farm boy says he's had enough
of milk cows running his life;
he talks about Minneapolis,
says that's where the money is,
so he's gone away to college,
plowing straight for an MBA.
My course is undecided.

It All
(For Michelle)

Sometimes it seems
her whole life has been one long ride
in the back seat of a car
traveling back and forth on this same highway;
and even now that she has a driver's license,
this two-lane highway beside the lake
is still the only road,
and it goes nowhere
she hasn't been ten thousand times.
She's bored by the curves of asphalt
she knows by heart,
the canyon walls of pine and spruce
that feed a claustrophobia in her soul.
Even the big blue lake that never shuts up,
its shimmering surface and far horizon
is a wall she can see through, but has no door.

She can't wait to get away
to It All,
the place the tourists come here
to get away from.
She'd settle for Duluth, finish high school there,
and then it's off to Vegas, baby,
where, she's heard, even a waitress
can pull down forty Gs easy
with a little cleavage and a smile,
like her friend's sister is doing.
Two more years and she's outta here,
unaware, at sixteen
that we build walls and fences,
draw boundaries and borders to surround ourselves
no matter where we are on the map we draw of our lives.

Between the Lines

On the corner of the envelope
her return address—
Toyota Corolla, New Mexico,
tells me that though not homeless,
she's on the road,
between adobe homes
in Albuquerque and Las Cruces.

She writes of making beer,
growing hops in flower pots,
finding work in a microbrewery
as a master brewer's apprentice.
Still undecided on her life's work,
she thinks she should settle on something
and why shouldn't that something be beer?

She writes that her lover's staying in Las Cruces,
working in a Barnes and Noble
while she and Peter, their big brown dog,
will move in with a new friend,
a woman with a Pomeranian,
a front porch and a garden,
the roads being congested with moving hearts.

Homeless in Duluth

I wish my ears
were big as elephant ears,
huge elephant ears
made of wool and flannel,
wool on the outside to cut the wind,
flannel on the inside, soft on my skin.
I'd wrap my big wool and flannel
elephant ears all around myself
and I wouldn't be cold tonight.

The Burden of Souls

On the highway north of Erzurum, Turkey,
migrating Kurds, traveling like gypsies,
on horseback, in ox and donkey carts
piled high with all they own;
bearded men, veiled women, shy children,
one girl carrying a rooster, walk beside this caravan,
dogs herding sheep, goats, cattle on their migration,
all captured in one black-and-white image.
I heard it said that these nomadic people
believe the camera has the power to steal their souls;
the angry expressions on the faces of the men,
hurling curses in Kurdish, confirming this.
Forty years later, I still have the picture of this caravan.
I wonder, how do I relieve myself of the burden of these souls,
the care of my own, being burdensome enough.

In Light Of

The same day
I saw a photo
of an old grandma
pushing an old grandpa
out of Sarajevo
in a wheelbarrow
my boss
bought a Lincoln Continental
about a block long
to transport
his over-the-belt belly
the twelve blocks
between his home and office.
I really didn't feel like riding
my bike twelve miles
to work and back today.
I could've driven;
but I felt a need
for self-righteousness,
misplaced, though it was,
in light of an old grandma
pushing an old grandpa
out of Sarajevo
in a wheelbarrow.

The Perfect Time

Enshrouded in a cloud of snow
kicked up by a county plow
on an icy road—
it's enough to scare the Zen into anyone,
not knowing if you've lived a minute
or a lifetime
inside this snowy nebula
or whether or not your tires are still on the road.
Only when you emerge
into transparent blue air, alive it seems,
and no other cars head-on in your lane,
do you think, damn, ain't this the perfect time
to begin your life anew.

Runaway Tractor

Lennon called it instant karma,
the preacher, reaping what you sow,
the judge says actions have consequences,
some simply say shit happens.
The poet says, talk about metaphor
slappin' your face,
kickin' your ass,
shakin' you awake
like your old man waking you for school;
metaphor gushing as the hose lets loose
from the tank of maple nectar,
the John Deere 2020, headed down the hill,
nobody at the wheel,
and no stoppin' it with prayers or curses,
all because you failed to set the brake,
put the tractor in gear,
chock the wheels, front and rear.

Barn

Rusty nails
with nothing to do in old age
but soak up sun,
protrude from the weathered oak ribs
of a sway-backed old barn,
think how it would be
to be silver and useful again,
holding tight a new wooden skin
that keeps at bay the wind
whistling through this rattling skeleton,
how it would be
for the barn to be filled up again,
warm beef in its belly,
dry hay in its head.

Cowbell

The rock 'n' roll bands
have taken all the cowbells
to add a rhythm to their sound.
Meanwhile, all the quiet cows
wander in the silent fog
with no way to be found.

One Way to Bridge a Cultural Divide

Just get an old backhoe
with a broken fan belt,
two guys,
one, an Anglo volunteer,
the other, a Hispanic mechanic,
a couple $^9/_{16}$th inch open-end wrenches,
a new fan belt that doesn't fit,
(install that one first)
and one that does.
After they scrape their knuckles on the fan,
fighting to make a belt that's too short, work,
have them talk like men talk—
to the belt, to the fan, the bolts, the wrenches,
words like "hijo de puta"
or "son of a bitch, this fucker won't fit"
and next thing you know
they're talking about their families and jobs,
baseball and winter storms
and when they finally get the belt installed,
end their conversation with high fives of success
as the backhoe growls back to life.

Perspective
(Cañones, New Mexico)

A rich woman
owns two houses in Cañones,
lives in one of them a few months a year
when she can get away from her career.
She drives by rusted trailer houses,
yards full of junk that is not junk,
saved for reasons unknown,
to reach her retreat
with the view of Pedernal and Tsiping Mesa.
Villagers peek out curtained windows
as she passes by in her new car,
wondering what it must be like
to be like her,
to live in busy Chicago
where the money seems to flow
like water released into the acequia,
then come to humble Cañones
on a bumpy, rutted road
to seek quiet and peace.
The people don't begrudge her what she has;
there have always been rich and poor,
but the irony is not lost on those
who have remained poor enough
to live in heaven all their lives,
somehow unable to leave.

Ghost Warriors

From a tribe I don't recognize,
these people with skin pink as a dog's belly,
climb the steps we carved in this red rock mesa
when ours was the only tongue spoken.
In those times, my tribe of farmer warriors
would not allow these intruders to pass,
spilling their blood before they reached our home.
Now we are gone as clouds that drop no rain,
our houses, even our sacred kiva crumbled by time.
Yet, the spirits of our warriors inhabit the cold wind,
raising dust that stings the eyes and soft skins
of these invaders, driving them back to the valley,
scurrying for highways and restaurants,
soft beds and churches;
while the warrior wind sings and laughs all night.

Kokopelli

The old trickster
plays his flute
all day,
all night;
the music, like wind
weaving buffalo grass,
and anyone can see,
that cat can dance, too.

Thousand-Year-Old Songs
(The music of Sharon Burch)

Her guitar strings,
the threads of a dream catcher,
gather wisps of old songs
sleeping on the wind
when her fingers begin to dance.
She sings songs
made up by a young Dineh girl
gathering dry piñon
from a waterless stream bed
a thousand years ago,
when hers was the people's only tongue.

Dull Knife's Blanket

What could be more honest
than Nebraska in February,
the ground barren,
cattle huddled in muddy pens,
dirty snow in ditches
and the lee of fence posts,
sandhill cranes not yet returned
to the fields along the Platte,
the sky, tattered and frayed,
sunset bloody as Dull Knife's blanket,
dragged from Sand Creek,
left in the hills above Ft. Robinson.

Reflection on a Starry Night

Driving south on U.S. 285
between Antonito and Tres Piedras,
Van Gogh's eyes reflect the night
in my rearview mirror.
Vincent's in the back seat
leaning his one ear against the window;
he appears to be ill, dizzy
from watching the universe spin.
I ask if I should drive him to a clinic—
Taos isn't far out of our way.
No. No, he says,
afraid I might become hypnotized
by what I see in his eyes,
Just watch for elk
crossing the goddamn highway.

A Place Called Ghost Ranch

Georgia O'Keefe, inscrutable, enigmatic
as some long-neglected goddess,
stares at me, unblinking, from a bookshelf,
perched there like a hunting owl.
Were I a mouse, scurrying
across the desert floor in moonlight,
I'd let her kill me if she had to
for the sake of art,
but only on the condition
she lay a cactus flower
beside my still-warm body,
before she begins painting
the skeleton she see inside me.

There is no questioning the motives
of gods, owls or artists, yet
I entreat the goddess,
as a last request,
to allow the artist to paint the sky
amethyst and indigo,
allow the owl to relentlessly ask its question,
though the answer has become irrelevant
to all but some curious poet,
not as alone as he presumed, in a library,
populated, at midnight, only by sleeping authors
on retreat at a place aptly called Ghost Ranch.

With a Nod to Georgia O'Keefe
(And the Grateful Dead)

I place scarlet begonia blossoms
in the empty eye sockets
of a sun-bleached cow's skull,
try to capture with camera
depth, angle, slant of light,
creep of shadow, color
and whatever is color's opposite;
making art of life and death,
as if art could take the place of breath
by scattering scarlet petals about,
already having begun to shrivel and wither.
The skull grins into the lens.

.

You Wish

He pulls up to the pump in his tan mini-van,
three screaming kids buckled in,
fills its tank and his lawn mower's gas can,
sighs at the rumble as a Harley revs up
at the next pump over,
almost cries as a blond in black leather
wraps her hair in a red bandana,
swings her long leg over the saddle,
hooks her fingers in some dude's belt loops,
looks right at him with eyes that say
ha, you wish!
roars out onto the highway.

Mars and Venus Meet on Earth TV

The weatherman on the nightly news
said get out and enjoy the weather,
a rare magnificent late autumn day.
Go fishing, he said. Play golf.
The newswoman, in response, said
it sounds like a perfect day
to wash the windows.

Jane Goodall
Grand Marshall 2013 Rose Parade

From the back seat of a convertible,
a little ol' lady in Pasadena
for New Years',
studies the hairless primates
lining the street.
She hopes, in time,
to communicate with this species.
She sees progress, already;
she waves,
they wave back.

The Lights Go Out During the Super Bowl

The announcers prattle on and on
about the lights dimming during the Super Bowl.
I think, why am I watching this crap?
and finding no reason but that the TV is on,
I pull a book from the bookcase,
open it randomly to a poem by Gary Snyder,
a poem about girls finding bear scat on a mountain trail,
not metaphorical scat, real bear shit on a real trail
and all that implies in the real world of women and men,
bears and berries, birth and death.
If you know Gary Snyder's poetry,
you know a poem about bear shit is not bullshit.
If Gary Snyder was here,
I would tell him, this is good shit!
Thanks, Gary.
I don't give a shit if the lights ever come back on.

Nobody Told Us About the Blues

You think your blues might be first generation,
brand new blues, if you grew up in the Cleaver's house
or the Nelson's or with the Partridge family.
Ward and June never taught their boys what to do with the blues,
never let on that white people get sick with the blues, too.
Ozzie Nelson never said a thing to his sons
about what hard times are like
and how they can hit you out of nowhere.
Mrs. Partridge never talked about Blacks or Hispanics
or how to relate to a Vietnamese immigrant
when your son didn't come home from the war.
Ozzie never mentioned cocaine to Ricky
so he found the white lady on his own.
Harriet and June never said much of anything except "dinner's ready."
They were never wrinkled, always permed, vacuumed in high heels;
you never heard them talk about what boys were after
or what makes little girls moan.
The Partridges never sang sad songs, much less the blues
and little Ricky was just a good-time rock 'n' roller.
They never sang about the life that stays on when the TV's turned off,
the stuff people gotta learn and learn good,
so that when the blue spotlight comes on,
shines on your sweating face,
and the band begins to cookin' on high heat, you can sing,
you have to sing, cause that's all you can do with the blues.